Note to Parents and Teachers

The READING ABOUT: STARTERS series introduces key science vocabulary to young children while encouraging them to discover and understand the world around them. The series works as a set of graded readers in three levels.

LEVEL 1: BEGINNING TO READ follows guidelines set out in the National Curriculum for Year 1 in schools. These books can be read alone or as part of guided or group reading. Each book has three sections:

• Information pages that introduce new words. These key words appear in bold throughout the book for easy recognition.
• A lively story that recalls this vocabulary and encourages children to use these words when they talk and write.
• A quiz and picture index ask children to look back and recall what they have read.

I KNOW THE WAY looks at ROUTES AND JOURNEYS. Below are some activities and answers related to the questions on the information spreads that parents, carers and teachers can use to discuss and develop further ideas and concepts:

p. 5 *Where might you fly in an aeroplane?* Aeroplanes are good for long journeys as they travel very fast. Ask children where they would like to fly to.

p. 7 *Why should you know your home and school addresses?* Knowing our address allows other people to help us find our way if we get lost.

p. 11 *What tall buildings might you spot in a city?* The tallest buildings are often in the centre of the city, such as banks, office blocks and hotels. You could also ask children what tall buildings they might find in smaller towns: e.g. church, mosque, town hall.

p. 13 *What features might you see on a walk in the country?* Take children out on a walk and encourage them to look for natural features: e.g. hill, lake, wood, cliffs or the sea. Point out these features on a map.

p. 15 *What else helps us stay safe when we cross a road?* Ask children to think of places near their school where it is safer to cross the road, e.g. zebra or pelican crossings, or at traffic lights, or where a lollipop man/woman helps them to cross the road.

p. 17 *What helps you to move around a school?* Corridors help us move through a building, stairs and lifts help us to move between floors. Signs tell us where to go.

p. 19 *How would you describe your home?* Ask children to think about what sort of building their home is, e.g. how old/large, what rooms it has, whether it has a yard.

p. 23 *Why do you think a globe is round?* Because our planet, Earth, is round!

ADVISORY TEAM

Educational Consultant
Andrea Bright – Science Co-ordinator, Trafalgar Junior School, Twickenham

Literacy Consultant
Jackie Holderness – former Principal Lecturer in Primary Education, Westminster Institute, Oxford Brookes University

Series Consultants
Anne Fussell – Early Years Teacher and University Tutor, Westminster Institute, Oxford Brookes University

David Fussell – C.Chem., FRSC

CONTENTS

© Aladdin Books Ltd 2006

Designed and produced by
Aladdin Books Ltd
2/3 Fitzroy Mews
London W1T 6DF

First published in
Great Britain in 2006 by
Franklin Watts
96 Leonard Street
London EC2A 4XD

A catalogue record for this
book is available from the
British Library.

ISBN 0 7496 6253 0

Printed in Malaysia

All rights reserved

Editor: Jim Pipe

Design: Flick, Book Design
and Graphics

Picture research:
Alexa Brown

Thanks to:
• The pupils of Darell Primary
School, Richmond-Upon-Thames,
for appearing as models in this book.
• Laura Khalil for helping to
organise the photoshoots.
• The pupils and teachers of
Trafalgar Junior School,
Twickenham and St. Nicholas
C.E. Infant School, Wallingford,
for testing the sample books.

Photocredits:
*l-left, r-right, b-bottom, t-top,
c-centre, m-middle*
Front cover tm & b, 3, 6, 7, 8tl &
mr, 16 both, 18, 20, 23, 24-25 all,
26-27 all, 28 both, 29bl, 30t,
32mlt, 32bl, 32mrb — Marc
Arundale / Select Pictures.
Front cover tr, 14br, 22b — istock-
photo.com. 2tl, 5b, 32tr — Corbis.
2ml, 14t — Brand X Pictures. 2bl,
19 both — DAJ. 4, 8bl, 12 —
Corel. 5t — Digital Stock. 10, 11t,
13tr, 31mr, 32ml — Flat Earth.
11br, 15, 17tr, 29tr, 31ml, 31br,
32mlb, mrt & mr — Photodisc.
21 — Sarah Bishop, African
Conservation Experience.

READING ABOUT

Starters

ROUTES AND JOURNEYS

I Know the Way

by Sally Hewitt

Aladdin/Watts

London • Sydney

What **journeys** do you make?
Some **journeys** are short.

You can walk to a place
that is **near** your home.

Some **journeys** are long.
They are too **far** to walk.

Train

You can ride
in a car or train.

You can fly in
an aeroplane.

Aeroplane

• Where might you fly in an aeroplane?

An **address** tells you where a place is.

This is Jon's **home**.

This is his **address**.
Jon knows his
address off by heart.

24 Green Lane
Newton
Kent
TN6 9DG

School

This is Jon's **school**.
It is near his **home**.

Part of the **school address** is the same as Jon's **home address**.

Junior School
South Road
Newton
Kent
TN6 5DT

• Why should you know your home and school addresses?

Jon walks to school with his Dad.

They walk past the **garage**.

They cross the **park**.

They turn left at the **shop**.

Jon's school is halfway down the road.

Jon always walks the same way to school. This is his **route**.

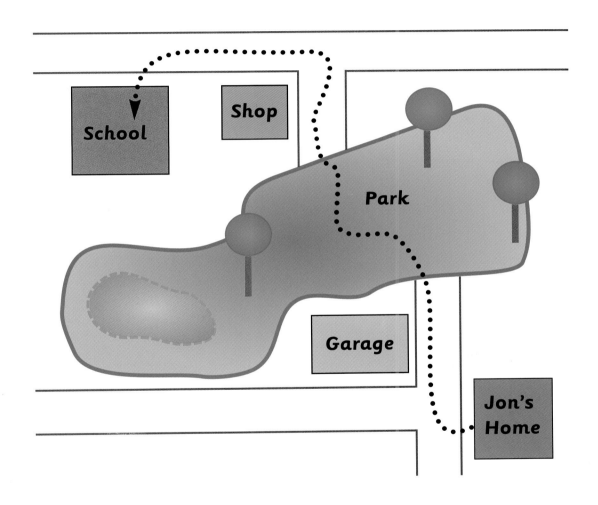

• Can you follow Jon's route to school with your finger?

Lee lives in a big city in a block of **flats**.

He can see other tall blocks from his window. These are **offices**.

Lee walks to school with his big sister.
They walk along busy **streets**.

They walk
past a market.

Lee can hear the
traffic roaring.

Baba lives on a farm.
She walks a long way to school.

Baba walks through the **trees**
and across the **fields**.

12

She crosses a **bridge** over the river.

Here is Baba's route to school.

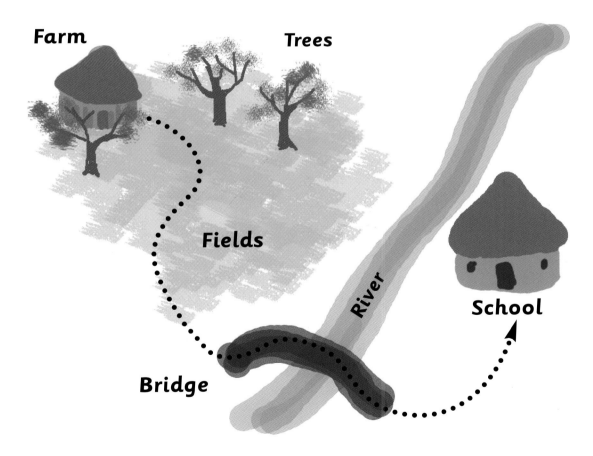

Farm

Trees

Fields

River

School

Bridge

• What features might you see on a walk in the country?

How do you **travel** to school?

Some children walk.
Some children **travel**
on the school bus.

Older children cycle.

14

It is important to stay **safe** near **roads**.

Always cross the **road** with an adult.
Look and listen.
Wait for the traffic to stop.
Then cross the **road safely**.

• What else helps us stay safe when we cross a road?

When Jon arrives
at school he walks
through the **gates.**

He meets his friends
and hangs up his coat
in the cloakroom.

They walk along the corridor to the **classroom**.

This is the route to Jon's **classroom**.

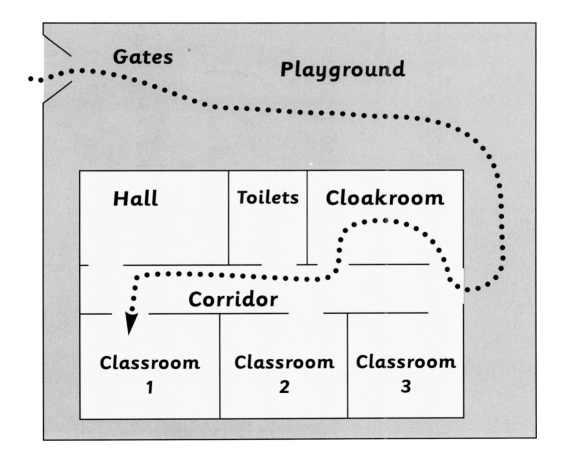

• What helps you to move around a school?

When you are walking along, look at the **buildings** around you.

Jon's school is **old**. It has brick walls and tall windows.

Lee's school is **new**.

It has concrete walls and wide windows.

Is your school like either of these schools?

- How would you describe your home?

At playtime, Jon and his friends
go into the **playground**.

They skip on the hard surface.
They climb on the climbing frame.

Tall trees shelter Baba's school
and **playground** from the hot sun.

At playtime, children run and skip
or rest in the shade.

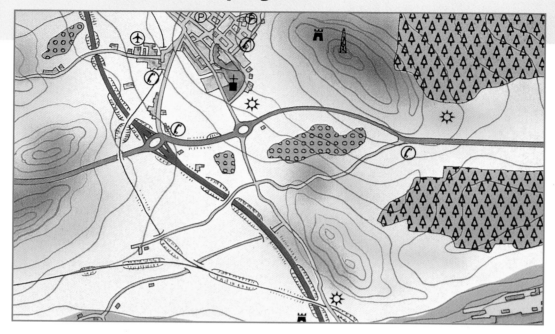

Map

Maps help you find the way.
Can you see the roads on this **map**?

You can find
where you are
and where
you want to
go on a **map**.

A **globe** is a **map** of the world.

Can you find where you
live on a **globe**?

• Why do you think a globe is round?

I KNOW THE WAY

Look out for words about **routes**.

Dad, Ada and Yin walk to **school**. It's not very **far**.

Every day, they take the same **route**.

They go through the **park**. They walk round the block of **flats**.

They pass Mrs Patel's **shop**. Mrs Patel waves.

They walk over the foot **bridge**
and turn right at the **garage**.

When they get to **school**,
Ada and Yin run through the **gate**.

They go into the **playground**
to meet their friends.

One day, Dad says, "Sally from next door is taking you to **school**."

Sally has a **map**. "We don't need a **map**," says Yin. "I know the way!"

"So do I!" says Ada.

They go through the **park**.

They walk round the block of **flats**.

"Do we turn left or right now?" asks Sally.
"Umm..." says Yin.

"Are we lost?" asks Sally.

Yin looks right.
Ada looks left.

Suddenly, Ada sees
Mrs Patel's **shop**.
"This way!"
she cries.

They pass the **shop** and Yin stops again. She scratches her head.

"What's your **school address?**" asks Sally.

Sally gets out her **map**.

"We can find your **school** on the **map**," says Sally.

The girls don't know their **school address**.

Then Yin sees the busy **road**. She sees the foot **bridge**.

"Look!" says Ada, "Here is the **bridge** on the **map**! And here is the **school**."

They go over the foot **bridge** and cross the **road safely**.

"There's the **garage**," says Yin. "We're very **near school** now."

"I can see it on the **map**," says Sally. "What a good thing you know the way!"

Draw your **route** to **school** or to your **classroom** from the **gates**. Follow it with your finger.

Talk about what you see on the way.

QUIZ

24 Green Lane
New ton
Kent
TN6 9DG

What does an **address** tell you?

Answer on page 6

What noises do you hear on city **streets**?

Answer on page 11

Why does Baba cross a **bridge**?

Answer on page 13

How do you cross the **road safely**?

Answer on page 15

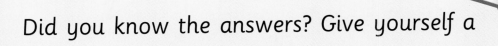

Did you know the answers? Give yourself a

Do you remember these words about **routes**?
Well done! Can you remember any more?

 journey
page 5

address
page 6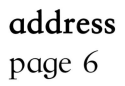

 route
page 8

street
page 11

 bridge
page 13

travel
page 14

 classroom
page 17

building
page 18

 playground
page 20

map
page 22